# DUTCH GENRE PAINTINGS
# IN HUNGARIAN MUSEUMS

MUSEUM OF FINE ARTS, BUDAPEST
ISTVÁN DOBÓ MUSEUM, EGER

# DUTCH GENRE PAINTINGS

*by Miklós Mojzer*

CORVINA PRESS

Translated by
EVA RÁCZ


Revised by
ELIZABETH WEST


Jacket, cover and typography by
LAJOS LENGYEL


Colour plates from the archives of Corvina Press, Budapest


Photo by
ALFRÉD SCHILLER

© Corvina 1967


Printed in Hungary
Kossuth Printing House, Budapest

The people of the Netherlands achieved a rare and enviable success in the early part o the seventeenth century. The seven provinces covering the area which is now Holland, with no aid from beyond their borders, liberated themselves from foreign domination. From that time onwards the people of Holland were able to see their native land with a new awareness.

The Dutch are fond of tranquillity and are devoted to the familiar objects which provide the background of their daily lives. Now their landscape painters discovered the beauty of the Dutch countryside. Though the country has none of the spectacular beauty seen in other parts of Europe, the Dutch painted their homeland with consummate art. With similar skill and care their portrait painters recorded the features of their fellow countrymen who were rarely exceptionally handsome. Although in Spain and Italy there was a much greater abundance of fruit, it was in Holland that the richest still lifes of fruit were composed whether on wood or canvas. Finally, the largest number of genre pictures were produced in the Netherlands although the social life of the country was without particular significance and indeed far from exemplary; nor were the clothes worn there in the Baroque period of particular interest.

Dutch painters displayed an objective, rather materialistic affection for their familiar environment which was almost the exclusive subject of their art.

In this part of the world we find, probably for the first time, evidence of the approach to art in which the artist looks at his subject without preconceived standards, attracted to it not because of an ideal quality he sees in it or a lesson to be learnt from it, but simply because he owns it. The genre paintings of the period show elemental pleasures—feasting, drinking, making merry with companions. Contemporary appreciation was based on a similar approach: to find delight in a work of art, to admire it without second thoughts.

In all Dutch painting there is an atmosphere of intimacy. It is the familiar atmosphere of everyday life: an uneventful life, with no suggestion of the solemnity of a special occasion. The genre painters had a gift for recording what was customary. The German word *Sittenbild* is very apposite.

The historical and sociological approach to art would lead us to expect works of historical reference from painters whose country had only just achieved national independence; a large number of paintings with historical themes were produced during the seventeenth century—in other countries. Dutch artists were not attracted to such themes and painted few works that record the history of their own times. In Dutch paintings of battles the theme is not war itself but only the episodes of war, the skirmishes, raids and highway robberies. Military parades or other celebrations were not favoured as subjects by the Dutch painters, but they liked to visit guardrooms. Peasants were shown in their homes, in the local inns, and when occasionally they were depicted at work this was the more domestic business of pig-killing with its suggestion of preparation for a family feast. Despite their obvious liking for everyday subjects, Dutch artists were not inspired by work, which had no special interest for them. As a subject for painting, one of the most industrious peoples of Europe devoted as little attention to peaceful endeavour as to military success.

Dutch merchants and tradesmen are depicted in many attitudes and in a variety of places—in the market, in the street, in taverns, and most frequently of all at home or visiting the homes of others; but they are rarely shown at work. There are few pictures of either shops or workshops. New buildings or scenes in the harbours and ports which were so important to the nation aroused very little interest in the artists of that period. The men and women they portrayed seemed to prefer their own homes where they were surrounded by familiar furniture, carpets, jugs and, last but not least, the paintings which reflected this daily background with such meticulous craftsmanship, if not with art. The Dutch paintings of this period reveal the people's fondness for precious materials and carefully preserved possessions. These paintings, which were produced in exceptional numbers, were intended to embellish the home and showed objects as the taste of the people dictated. Still lifes, landscape or genre paintings could be found in any house except the house of prayer. In their strict Protestantism the churches were devoid of all pictorial decoration. The artist who can be said to represent a culture which was largely Protestant and middle-class rarely ventured to attempt anything outside his own immediate experience. The masters of genre painting proved to be strikingly clumsy when they essayed allegorical or mythological subjects: this was a sphere in which they were no longer "at home."

It seems that it was in Dutch genre paintings that man was first shown without the support of any myth, in which men and women were seen as lovers of art, masters of their environment and unaffected by legend. Genre pictures usually lack all literary reference as well as historical significance. Of all types of art, Dutch genre painting is the most difficult to classify according to the concepts rooted in European humanism. Genre painting has no iconography, no theory, nor was it based on any earlier style known to the history of painting. One might say it is a genre of "low origins."

In the earliest examples of genre painting, in the sixteenth century, the artists took their themes from the fairground, market place and kitchen. They had an abundance of the good things of life and acquired desirable possessions with the fresh delight of the newly rich. We find a new element in their work in that they could now exercise choice in the subject of their paintings, whereas formerly they had been presented with religious and mythological themes ready made. And the choice usually fell upon individual objects which appealed to them because they were beautiful or picturesque. This was the period when all subjects were considered equally suitable for representation, human figures and their environment, or the animal and vegetable world. Man himself became an object like any other when chosen for representation by the artist; thus there was in the sixteenth century a close relationship between still-life and genre painting. In Holland, Pieter Aartsen and his pupil, Joachim Beuckelaer, were two of the first artists to paint both still lifes and genre paintings. In their works the individual, who until then had dominated the European paintings in which he appeared, now seemed to merge with his background. The complexity of personality was not indicated: people merely occupied a place in the world perceived by the artist. Types were more important than individuals at this time—peasants, soldiers, members of the petit bourgeoisie or of the upper middle classes. The masters of genre painting preferred average men and women.

As the peasant preceded the bourgeois in society so he was represented in painting long before the bourgeois was put on canvas. The figure most typical of genre painting is that of the peasant, who neither as a creative artist nor as the subject of art has individual features. Wherever he appeared it was always as a type. The peasant cannot be seen apart from his occupation and the narrow confines of his environment. It therefore follows almost naturally that one of the greatest, if not the greatest, genre painter was the artist who depicted peasants, Pieter Bruegel the elder. The portraits of Flemish villagers left to posterity by "Peasant Bruegel" are so impressive and powerful, their appeal so universal and timeless, that they rank with the greatest masterpieces of the Italian Renaissance. The Dutch masters, however, were far less ambitious. Their horizon was narrow, or rather artificially limited. Instead of the epic landscapes which form the background of Bruegel's pictures we see in the Dutch pictures of peasants in the seventeenth century, dark interiors, untidy and bare, sharply contrasting with the homes of the middle classes which are shown as well-furnished, clean and orderly. But the homes of the villagers, whether large or small, are like disorderly barns or mere hovels. The peasants who live in them are coarse, often churlish, humorous and uncultured folk, living in an uninhibited manner according to their instincts. They are primitive people representing the average of their kind. The carefully arranged homes of the middle classes show that their owners are rational beings who think about their actions, while the peasants—with the free and thoughtless manner of their lives—are shown against a dark and disorderly background. It was thus that the peasants were shown in the work of Adriaen Brouwer, born and educated in Holland, but who later, of all Dutch painters, was most consistently within the tradition of Flemish Baroque art.

It is noticeable that the peasants in Dutch genre paintings are depicted as being more vulgar than those represented in this anecdotal type of picture by the artists of other countries. None of the painters of feudal Spain, nor the artists who lived among the Italian aristocracy, nor the French Le Nain brothers, indeed none of the most distinguished masters of the late Baroque, depicted the peasant as

8

such a low creature as did the bourgeois artists of Holland. In these paintings, however, there is no attempt to present a preconceived notion of bucolic and idyllic peasant life which had no existence in reality. To these artists, peasant life was simply an interesting subject to be painted. It was pleasant for members of the bourgeoisie, whose social position was becoming increasingly secure, to regard the tillers of the soil as primitive and crude beings, whose merry antics they could observe as they might watch mischievous children at play. The finest examples of urban genre paintings and the most original of the anecdotal paintings of peasants were executed with similar intentions on the part of the artist: in each case he wanted to present a situation and to depict his figures as boisterous, happy or, at the very least, contented. Tragedy and bitterness were shunned by both the Dutch and Flemish genre painters. The main difference between the two seems to depend on the fact that the Flemish sense of humour is expressed in action while the humour of the Dutch paintings depends on a particular humorous situation. Peasants and members of the bourgeoisie alike have every appearance of enjoying themselves in the scenes depicted. In some respects the peasant background was like that of a middle-class citizen but without a landlord; and indeed, by the end of the seventeenth century the peasant types were becoming more and more similar to the middle-class types.

The rapid development of Dutch genre painting was mainly due to the wealth of the new middle class, and more generally to the whole development of a middle-class economy. Until now the most important patrons of art in the country, neither Church nor secular powers felt the need for genre paintings, nor was there any demand for these from less powerful bodies such as town councils; Dutch genre pictures are therefore unburdened with any extraneous ideological messages. The genre paintings belonged to a single home for which they were specially bought; they were not commissioned as were the altarpieces, frescoes and palace decorations acquired elsewhere. Pictures began to have value as a precious commodity, and were usually smaller than the panels until then in vogue in other countries. The painters were uncommitted to authority and equally uninterested in the will, wishes and aspirations of the people they portrayed. In the genre paintings man becomes a denizen of the earth. In the Dutch interiors a man of the middle classes is linked to his environment as surely as the peasant to his. The figures are very often passive characters in the scene. The 'plot' disappears amidst the details and together with the plot the individual participating in the events also vanishes; the hero becomes a model.

Seen in relation to European Baroque art Dutch genre painting assumed a 'heretic' quality, for it was in this type of work that Dutch painters moved furthest away from all earlier traditions and from the religious paintings of their own times. In the Netherlands, genre painting developed as an independent style, whereas in Italy, it did not become completely divorced from religious and mythological works. Parables from the gospels provide the themes for Domenico Feti's splendid genre paintings. There is a visionary quality in his picture of 'the blind leading the blind.' In Caravaggio's art man is a giant when compared with the mortal being of northern art, a giant who demands space for the expression of his dramatic intensity. Up to the end of the eighteenth century Italian genre paintings suggest the influence of the theatre or some nobleman interested in peasant ways. It is true that Jan Steen also learned something from the contemporary stage but nevertheless the lesson failed to have a decisive impact on his work. The Dutch genius expresses itself in craftsmanship, thinks in everyday terms and is most eminently suited to genre painting.

It was scarcely possible in the seventeenth century to escape the influence of Italian art but though the Dutch gained inspiration from their knowledge of it their art was not decisively affected by it. The masters who worked beside Pieter van Laer (Bamboccio) in Rome during the first third of the century remained characteristically Dutch in spite of Caravaggio's influence in the Eternal City where the Baroque was just beginning to develop. Painters from Utrecht and Haarlem took home as much as they could absorb of the achievements of artists in Rome, but once at home they adapted what they had seen, and created works that were typically Dutch. Similarly there was not one single Italian painter in whose work there was the same objectivity and popular realism as that found in Dutch painting; nor could they touch vulgar themes with the same spontaneity and lack of deliberation. Only Giuseppe Maria Crespi had something in common with the Dutch, but this was much later and not quite independent of any Dutch or Flemish influence. The informality, simplicity and frankness essential to genre painting are apparently northern traits. Just as in the seventeenth and eighteenth centuries Italian and Spanish genre painting could not deny its aristocratic ancestry and portraits of saints and noblemen continued to be esteemed more highly than genre painting, so Dutch genre painting could not deny its peasant origins.

Renaissance and Baroque art widened the scope of painting in regard to iconography, but it was the Dutch painting which brought about a revolution by replacing abstract formulas by a matter-of-fact artistic conception of the world. Dutch artists painted the colourful and changing detail of their own world. In the pictures of Vermeer van Delft the background is nearly always confined to one corner of a room. In those of Pieter de Hoogh we see the detail of interiors subtly illuminated by the filtered rays of the pure light from without. In these interiors the colours are made strangely vivid by the sunlight which also intensifies the shadows on the objects portrayed and almost seems to magnify them, as if to enable them to be more thoroughly analysed. As experiments in the painting of light Vermeer's work was unequalled in his age. When compared with the interiors lit by candles or torches which had been favoured earlier, particularly in Utrecht, Vermeer's pictures of home life were classic in their tranquillity. In the work of the master of Delft we find some of the finest achievements in the history of genre painting. In some of his pictures he ventured to transcend the narrower limits of this type of painting, and the scenes depicted became imbued with a significance beyond their immediate reality. Thus in his picture entitled *Atelier*, a masterpiece in the Kunsthistorisches Museum in Vienna, he summed up his *ars poetica* on a high artistic level, unequalled by any other genre painter of his time. The quality of realism in this picture differs from that in genre paintings by other artists. The subject is idyllic, aspiring to the ideal; the pictorial effect is crystalline and somewhat dazzling. It is a composition of elusive colours, delicate effects of light and shadow in which there is a scarcely perceptible dividing line between a marvellous reality on the one hand, and a visionary quality of dream on the other. The scene hovers on the brink of everyday simplicity and allegorical solemnity. One is surprised by the directness of its impact before realizing the care with which the subject has been presented. In Vermeer's art there is poetry and an intimation of the ideal; his approach is that of the artist who begins with an idea. It is an approach in strange contrast to the attitude of most genre painters of that period. In a later work *The Allegory of Faith* (New York) Vermeer himself was not very successful in his attempt to give the painting a meaning beyond its immediate reality. In such attempts he found himself alone among his compatriots.

Among all the great masters of Dutch painting there was this same peculiar detachment which made them diverge from the prevailing trend. The hint of bitterness in the portraits of Frans Hals, the emotional power of the later Rembrandt, whose isolation increased as his popularity waned, are completely alien to the world of Gabriel Metsu or Ter Borch from whose works the late period of Dutch genre painting developed. Like Vermeer, Frans Hals and Rembrandt transcended the limitations of any one style. Genre painting was greatly influenced by the work of Frans Hals but few of his own genre paintings are known and these few are not typically Dutch; and Rembrandt's genre pictures belong so much to the world of the Bible that they cannot at all be compared to the genre paintings of his day. Vermeer's paintings, comparatively few in number, remained for long unknown: Houbraken, the most important chronicler and biographer of seventeenth-century Dutch painting, did not even mention Vermeer's name. In these circumstances the personality of the painter merged into the rich background of his times, and became as vague and unidentifiable as the figures in the conversation pieces.

The golden age of Dutch genre painting lasted only for about fifty years. By the beginning of the

12

eighteenth century it was already losing some of its early vigour. In its later phase of *Feinmalerei*, the quality that earlier had given it a kinship with still life became overlaid with virtuoso technique. The Dutch middle classes developed a taste for the habits of the aristocracy. The exceedingly wealthy homes now portrayed had none of the homeliness of the earlier middle-class interiors, and it seemed that true gallantry was lacking in their inhabitants. In the earlier pictures gestures were rarely used and had little significance, but in this later phase gestures were used in an attempt to give individuality to the figures. Thus it is in genre painting that we first sense the decline of Dutch painting. The great period of landscape and still-life painting lasted much longer, although both still-life and genre painting originated in the same period, almost two hundred years prior to the decay of the latter.

This book is based almost exclusively on a study of the Dutch genre paintings in the Budapest Museum of Fine Arts. An exception is the Terbrugghen picture in the István Dobó Museum at Eger, the only notable work by any of the followers of Caravaggio in Utrecht.

Terbrugghen lived in Italy for ten years and when he returned to Holland in 1614 he had learned a great deal from the work and outlook of Caravaggio and his circle. Of all the Dutch artists who stayed in Italy for any length of time Terbrugghen had the most powerful personality. Apart from his outstanding religious works it was chiefly because of his genre painting that he became famous (Plate 1). One glance at his pictures shows that he was not a painter of the Dutch milieu; the dark, natural background of his pictures with large figures and the dress worn by the figures which invariably occupy a large proportion of the canvas show that he preferred the Italian style. He depicts figures in taverns, brothels and soldiers' haunts; the colours are vivid, the detail clear. When compared with the work of Italian artists influenced by Caravaggio, Terbrugghen's pictures are crude, objective and reveal an inclination for vulgar pleasures. He was a fine colourist and in his day the most consistent master of fine light effects in Holland. We are bound to look upon him as the only Dutch painter who successfully transplanted the *grandezza* of Italian art into the artistic idioms of his native land. True, his own career did not follow the trend of Dutch art, but he was the first artist of note to see and put on canvas something of the light and colour effects achieved by Vermeer. An early death at the age of only forty-one left his promise unfulfilled. His contemporary, Pieter Lastman, who painted biblical and historical themes, and who had also been educated in Rome, and was a student member of the Elsheimer circle, was more fortunate in providing for his artistic succession: he taught Rembrandt.

Pieter van Laer should also be mentioned as one of the Dutch artists who spent some time in Rome. His *Landscape with Morra-Players* (Plate 2) now in the Budapest Museum of Fine Arts was painted in Italy where the artist lived surrounded by a lively group of friends until, sick and with only a few more years to live, he returned to his native Haarlem. The figures in his pictures are shown in the open air—outlaws, labourers, smugglers, beggars, travellers, villagers and soldiers. Laer carried with him the memory of northern types divorced from their own background, and when he returned his vision was enriched by his experience of Italian Baroque light effects and the more informal style of representation he had seen in Italy. Laer was a rather tragic figure whose originality and artistic style brought him attention from the increasingly important art circles of the Eternal City where he was much better known and respected than in his native land. Fellow artists in Holland found nothing remarkable in his work for they favoured a style that was more objective, dispassionate and analytical. Nevertheless it was to Laer that Philips Wouwerman owed his own achievement in developing that type of genre painting of which he is one of the most outstanding exponents—landscape with figures. From 1640 onwards he painted many notable genre pictures of this type.

Haarlem was one of the principal places in which Dutch genre painting developed. It was there that most of the painters included in this volume received their training and were encouraged to pursue a characteristically Dutch style of genre painting. One of the chief sources of inspiration was the studio of Frans Hals where Wouwerman, mentioned above, and later Jan Miensz Molenaer, Adriaen van

Ostade and, of course, Dirck Hals, his brother and Harmen Hals, his son, were either pupils or assistants. Pieter de Molyn, Dirk Maas and Ostade's pupil, Cornelis Bega, were also natives of Haarlem, while between 1612 and 1617 Willem Buytewech, born in Rotterdam, was also active there.

The picture by Buytewech now in Budapest (Plates 4 and 5) dates from this period and admirably illustrates the artist's indebtedness to Frans Hals. His influence can be seen in the use of bright, lively colours and the evidence of a keen observation tinged with humour. Of course, the figures in Frans Hals's conversation pieces are more sharply and profoundly characterized than Buytewech's well-dressed citizens, here seen for the first time against a rather restricted background showing only a small section of one of the rich and intimate interiors so much appreciated by the Dutch. Hals and the painters of early conversation pieces still limited the extent of the interiors they depicted, especially when these were furnished. Buytewech's work also illustrates very well the independence and freedom from tradition of the genre: it would be very difficult indeed to find the direct antecedents of this painting. Though one of the earliest of the genre paintings, it is nevertheless one of the most comprehensive examples of a style which was just beginning to develop rapidly and along many different lines. Scarcely more than a dozen of his works are known to us.

These were the years when genre painting was fashionable throughout Europe. It was the period when Velazquez painted what are known as his *bodegones*, among them his *The Breakfast* now in the Budapest Museum of Fine Arts. There is also in the Budapest Museum of Fine Arts an example of early Flemish genre painting, a work by Sebastian Vrancx which depicts a group of people at a feast. Jan Liss, almost exactly contemporary with Buytewech, was born in Oldenburg, studied in Amsterdam and later settled in Italy. It was probably in Amsterdam that he painted the *Village Wedding Procession* which has found its way to Budapest. There are signs of Flemish influence in this work but the later paintings by Liss are firmly rooted in the Italian tradition from which they gain a certain quality of nobility. For this he was partly indebted to Caravaggio but also to Domenico Feti, one of the pioneers of Italian genre painting at that time. Feti died in 1623, one year before Buytewech.

Frans Hals's brother, Dirck, was a more mannered exponent of the style of genre painting developed in Frans's studio than was Buytewech who was in Haarlem for only five years. The jovial company seen in Dirck's picture (Plates 6 and 7) provide an impressive subject: the people seem to have suspended their merrymaking specially for the purpose of posing for a group portrait. However, their seeming casualness does not succeed in conveying the powerful and accurate characterization of the figures which was Dirck Hals's intention. But the pictures are rich in colours and his treatment of clothes and especially of lace is evidence of great technical mastery. Whereas Dirck apparently preferred better middle-class society, Frans Hals's son, Harmen frequently painted the amusements of the humbler classes, for instance, in his *Peasants at a Wedding Feast* (Plate 8). The puppet-like figures and the scene itself recall the work of Frans Hals, but this painting is more like a simplified version of one of the father's pictures, and the vigour characteristic of the latter is lacking in the work of his son.

Jan Miensz Molenaer also worked in Frans Hals's studio and it were probably Frans Hals's early religious works, most of them now lost, from which he derived the idea for his *Peter's Denial of Christ* (Plates 9 and 10). It is a strange representation of the subject for at first glance the figures seem more like a group of travelling players in a village tavern than characters from the Bible. However, all such doubts must be dispelled because of the care with which the details of the story have been portrayed: the dwarf-like figure warming himself by the fire, the servant-girl who exposes Peter, Peter himself ready to slip away unnoticed, and the cock in the yard. Here there is no attempt to treat the theme in a lofty way: it is purely descriptive. Yet the artist fails to deal with a biblical subject, a failure shared by most of the Dutch masters with the exception of Rembrandt. Jan Steen's religious pictures often verge on the comical and are sometimes quite laughable. Dutch painting was basically genre-like and always, excepting Rembrandt, Dutch painters failed in any attempt to transcend the limitations of the genre just as Italian and Spanish portrait painters could not free themselves from the spell of mythicism and humanism. Molenaer was a dedicated genre painter, equally fertile in the production of bourgeois and peasant scenes. The figures in his earlier works are robustly portrayed and full of character but in his later pictures there is a tendency towards *Feinmalerei*.

There is less evidence of the influence of Frans Hals in Adriaen van Ostade's figures than in those of Molenaer. Ostade was one of the truly great painters of the century and his work owes little to the immediately preceding generation of artists. Of the many hundreds of paintings which he completed some are examples of bourgeois genre painting and others exemplify every kind and variety of the peasant genre. It is difficult, if not foolish, to attempt to pick out the principal works of so vast an output; however, the Budapest *Interior with a Peasant Family* (Plate 23) is one example of his many excellent works. There are no sensitive individual portraits among the peasants he portrayed nor have they any of the qualities we have learned to call beautiful or worthy of emulation. Peasant conditions, formerly so miserable, had improved by the middle of the seventeenth century, and the artist fills in the details of the peasant world without compassion or criticism. The family group in the Budapest picture is objectively portrayed, and there is a marvellous spontaneity in the movements of the figures. It is a profoundly realized portrayal of family affection, shown without sentimentality, the figures merging naturally into the background which is of equal importance to the composition. Adriaen's brother and pupil, Isack, was his junior by ten years; he died at the early age of twenty-eight but he recorded during his short life scenes of peasant life which have the same originality and technical excellence as those of his brother. The example of his work reproduced here (Plate 24) is a typical representation of that popular subject, pig-killing. This is a theme closely associated with the peasant genre. Even in very early Dutch paintings a disembowelled pig was used as the focal point of the composition: it was used for the first time in 1551 by Marten van Cleve in his *Flayed Ox* (Kunsthistorisches Museum, Vienna), and it was again used in 1563 by Joachim Beuckelaer in his *Slaughtered Pig* (Wallraf-Richartz Museum, Cologne). Quite two generations later Rembrandt used a similar motif in his pictures of ox carcasses in the butcher shops (Paris, Budapest). In some of the works of the elder van Ostade—for example in his *The Quill-Sharpener* (Plate 21)—there is a hint of striving after the kind of effect achieved by Rembrandt; and in Isack van Ostade's *Pig-Killing* in Budapest (Plate 25) there are also traits reminiscent of Rembrandt, for example in the use of light and shade and the predominantly brownish tone of the painting.

Another Haarlem painter worthy of mention is Pieter de Molyn to whom one of the paintings reproduced in this volume is generally attributed (Plates 17 and 18). His canvas features large figures of peasants in the foreground and is for this reason very different from most of the pictures we have included; it is the work of a man with a generous and intimate understanding of peasants and their ways.

Andries Both was yet another artist who left Holland for Italy; like Terbrugghen, he was an Utrecht pupil of Abraham Bloemaert in Rome. The picture by him in the collection of the Budapest Museum of Fine Arts (Plate 3) was painted before he left Holland. His contrasts of light and shade are ample proofs of his training amidst the Romanists in Utrecht, while his manner of representing his vulgar theme identifies him as a contemporary, of Frans Hals. Jacob Duck also studied in Utrecht and later was active in The Hague; he specialized in scenes from military life (Plate 15).

Joost Cornelisz. Droochsloot was one of the many lesser genre painters. He celebrated his eightieth birthday in Utrecht and when he died in 1666 he had completed a great number of figure paintings. One of his pictures in the Budapest Museum of Fine Arts has a biblical subject: a procession of the sick is seen walking towards an imagined Lake Bethesda. In another picture he seems to have assembled the entire population of a village in an unintegrated but carefully executed composition (Plate 19).

It would be difficult to consider Rembrandt for inclusion in an album of genre paintings. His own genre paintings, and even his etchings, are quite different from all other works. If we apply the inclusion of the human figure as a criterion for the classification of genre paintings—a justifiable view—then, for instance, we must include his *Butcher's Shop*, a late work now in the Louvre, for the figure of a woman can be seen leaning forward from the door behind the staircase in the background;

it is true that she is only a very subsidiary figure, but she is certainly present. However, there are no figures in the earlier *Butcher's Shop* painted in the late sixteen-thirties and now in Budapest. In this splendid composition the artist uses layers of glaze to suggest the stiffening carcasses of the animals and lumps of suet, and sets an array of tools and implements against a glimmering, greenish background, but these details merely suggest the proximity of man and his work without showing him directly. We would be even less justified in calling this painting a still life, for it is more markedly different from what we usually think of as still life than from genre painting in which pig-killing was at least a customary theme. Isack van Ostade's *Slaughtered Pig* in Budapest (Plate 24) clearly indicates that the artist's interest lay only in genre painting, and in his treatment of the subject he is greatly influenced by his knowledge of Rembrandt's work. Nor is Rembrandt's *Old Rabbi* (Plate 27) unquestionably a genre painting; it is more like a portrait, but it is more than a portrait. The work of Rembrandt defies classification, either as a whole or in detail. And what we have said about Dutch painting in general has scarcely any truth in relation to the work of Rembrandt, the greatest artist of them all. In his *Old Rabbi* the background is quite different from anything one usually finds in genre painting, and it is only in the position of the figure, timeless and universal in its quiet thoughtfulness, that the picture has a link with genre painting.

There are relatively few genre paintings by Rembrandt's pupils, Dou, Eeckhout and Nicolaes Maes, but these are all in the style of the master. The picture of an officer of the Leiden Civic Guard by Gerrit Dou (Plate 28), whose work is often too self-confident and over-refined, is just as delicately balanced between portraiture and genre painting as Rembrandt's *Old Rabbi*. Dou's work reveals all the care for detail and matter-of-fact rendering of a man with a particular gift for accurate representation. In this picture he has surrounded the figure with a number of mysteriously illuminated and indistinctly outlined objects in the same way that portrait painters, according to the general demand of the middle class, used a curtain to frame the subject.

The composition of Eeckhout's *Scholar with his Books* (Plate 30) shows the influence of the later

Rembrandt. This is a true genre painting. It is clearly based to some extent on the *Old Rabbi* which later made its way to Budapest and which Eeckhout may have seen when this was still in the master's studio and Eeckhout himself only twenty-one.

Jan Victors, who was born about 1620 and died in 1676, was one of Rembrandt's lesser known pupils. A contemporary of Eeckhout, he joined Rembrandt's studio around 1635, perhaps even earlier than Eeckhout. He was far from being a genius and his life was a hard one. He tried to make a living by giving nursing assistance to families stricken by the plague, and he died during a voyage to the East Indies where he was hoping to retrieve his fortunes. His style, compared with that of his contemporaries, was coarse, vulgar and declamatory. He based his genre paintings on stories from the Bible, and he also painted heavily humorous conversation pieces. Examples of both can be seen in the Budapest Museum of Fine Arts, the most original of them all being perhaps his *Market Scene with a Quack at his Stall* (Plate 29). This was painted about 1650 but the style and manner of presentation are those of an earlier period. This was the beginning of the great period of middle-class genre painting when artists were developing a style quite different from Victors' over-familiar anecdotical approach .In the late sixteen-fifties Nicolaes Maes was painting his finest conversation pieces in Dordrecht and Vermeer was at work on his early masterpieces. Gabriel Metsu settled in Amsterdam in 1655, the commencement of what proved to be his best period; and Gerard ter Borch had been recognized in Deventer since 1654 as an outstanding portrait and genre painter. Unfortunately we know of no genre pictures in Hungary by any of these artists. However, there are good examples of the work of two of the very greatest of them all, Pieter de Hoogh and Jan Steen, in the Budapest Museum of Fine Arts.

Pieter de Hoogh's best period encompassed about a decade, and his *Lady Reading a Letter* (Plate 31) in the Budapest Museum was painted during the last years of this great phase. The influence of Vermeer is obvious in the style and technique of the picture which was probably painted towards the end of the artist's stay in Delft, or else immediately after he moved to The Hague. The atmosphere of shallow superiority and artificiality which was later to indicate the waning powers of the artist's imagination is not evident here. This picture is one of those many works which depict the middle-class home in the absence of the master: the viewer is reminded with nostalgia of his own home as he looks at the clean and restful interior. Nothing disturbs the calm of the scene; there is no suggestion of work, noise or possible disturbance, and the tranquil landscape seen through the window gives the impression that this calm extends far beyond the four walls of the room.

Jan Steen, also a painter of middle-class genre, was possessed of a livelier personality than that of Pieter de Hoogh. He was a prolific artist, but the standard of his work was far from constant. However, like Adriaen van Ostade, he can be credited with several dozen significant works. He liked to paint his fellow-citizens enjoying themselves with their companions, eating and drinking, arguing or quarrelling, at home, in the streets or with the bawdy hostesses of some ill-famed tavern. Of all the genre painters he was the most gifted as a portrayer of character. His figures are not mere types: they are individuals, men and women with definite personalities. He had an inexhaustible interest in human character and the infinite variety of human situations. If an artist can ever be said to be on intimate terms with the spectator of his work, then that artist is Jan Steen. His work is a veritable encyclopaedia of the way of life of the Dutch middle classes and petit bourgeoisie. He usually depicts an indoor incident so that he can show the movements and relationship between individual figures, yet without adding any flavour of literary affectation to the work. Two of his pictures are reproduced in this volume (Plates 34–37). One of these is one of his most ambitious works and contains a self-portrait. In the minds of the younger generation Jan Steen was already a figure of romance about whom anecdotes circulated, more probably because of the content of his pictures than because he in fact led an interesting life.

Caspar Netscher had already become a pupil of Gerard ter Borch sometime during the sixteen-fifties and he was the pupil who most successfully emulated the style of his master. As a young man he made excellent copies of a number of Ter Borch's works. The painting in the Budapest Museum of Fine Arts entitled *Guard Room with Trumpeter* can probably be attributed to him for it is very similar in composition to a painting done by Ter Borch in 1658. It has also been suspected that the *Presentation of the Medallion* (Plate 32) is an adaptation of a painting by Ter Borch; it was probably painted during the sixteen-fifties. Although it is typical of the best of Netscher's work, the somewhat affected gesture foreshadows the approach of the later more mannered period of genre painting.

The trend of the later period is best represented by *The Chess Players* (Plate 33) by Cornelis de Man of Delft, who lived to see the eighteenth century. He spent several years in Italy and France, an experience from which he did not greatly benefit for when he returned home he produced works with an abundance of detail, chiefly conversation pieces depicting middle-class life, in the manner of Vermeer and Pieter de Hoogh.

Study tours in Italy were fashionable among Dutch artists throughout the seventeenth century. Interestingly enough, however, the very greatest of the Dutch artists were the very ones who did not go there. Neither Frans Hals, Vermeer, Pieter de Hoogh, Rembrandt nor Jan Steen ever visited Italy. Nor did the Ostades ever find their way to that sunnier land. Though there was an Italian-inspired peasant genre as well as the typically Dutch peasant genre, the middle-class genre had no such link with Italy where there was nothing resembling this kind of painting.

In the mid-sixteen-forties Nicolaes Berchem returned to Haarlem still spellbound by the charm of the Italian landscape and its inhabitants. He spent a much shorter period of time in Rome than had Pieter Laer who died in Haarlem in the same year that Berchem set out from there. Berchem was chiefly a landscape painter, but he also painted mythological works and made studies of animals. In his work he portrays southern types, and his idyllic pastoral scenes are quite unlike the work of his contemporaries who were at home only when painting their native landscape. His polished style, use of colour and remote classicism were at once the virtues and defects of his work. He rarely seems to have painted real peasants, only a general type: he painted "the People." Shepherds and shepherdesses, in landscapes made interesting by rocks and groves or ruins, constituted his main subjects. In contrast to these gently pastoral scenes the work of his pupil, Dirk Maas, depicts more eventful open-air scenes, of skirmishes, hunting and crowds at the fair (Plate 40). He too painted Italian scenes and made etchings; and he was almost as interested in painting fine horses as Wouwerman.

Like his contemporaries, Adriaen van Ostade and Gerrit Dou, Berchem was hard-working and prolific and remained active throughout his life. Lights which emphasized the smooth surfaces, deep shadows and subtle details of the drawing contributed to the popularity of the paintings and etchings of Berchem who was later active in Amsterdam. Of his pupils, Pieter de Hoogh became one of the great masters, and Jacob Ochtervelt painted middle-class genres and portraits. A painting in Budapest by Ochtervelt is dated 1670 (Plate 38).

Dominicus van Wynen went to Italy from Amsterdam, and when in Rome, adopted the high-sounding pseudonym of Ascanius. He is a little-known artist; apart from the picture reproduced in this volume there is a record of only one other signed work by him. The picture in Budapest (Plates 41–43) is a late work that would have been appreciated by that gay and sometimes ironically-minded circle of northern masters in Rome which earlier centred round Pieter van Laer. For Laer's approach to genre painting persisted into the second half of the century; it was a journalistic approach, as if the artist went out in search of a subject, roaming the streets and market-places, lingering in taverns, houses and courtyards. It was an approach which reached its culmination in the work of Philips Wouwerman, also a native of Haarlem. The horse, seen as the friend of man as well as a conveyance for him on his travels, became for Wouwerman an important theme which he treated in a variety of ways. Horses are shown in the innumerable situations in which they are employed by men—on their journeys, when hunting and on excursions (Plate 39). It is characteristic of the majority of genre painters that they avoid outdoor scenes; Wouwerman on the contrary avoided interiors. He cannot strictly be regarded as a genre painter: he excels as a landscape painter, and he has a gift for peopling his landscape with figures as vividly alive as the family circles and festive groups painted by Jan Steen.

Wouwerman developed into one of the great masters, contributing to our knowledge of Dutch life with his landscapes of a typically Dutch countryside.

An even closer connection with Laer can be seen in the work of Thomas Wyck of Haarlem, who was a pupil of Laer. Wyck also visited Italy where he painted landscapes and townscapes. Later he became more interested in genre. The lively action in the characteristic work reproduced in this volume (Plates 44 and 45) indicates how much the artist profited from his studies in Italy, and the picture is an outstanding example of his art.

The last three artists whose work is reproduced in this volume were also natives of Haarlem and all three of them were pupils of Adriaen van Ostade. Cornelis Bega was one of the first generation of Ostade pupils. His work was scarcely affected by his sojourn in Italy; throughout his short life he worked very closely in the style of his master, but his pictures were more superficial, like much of the work of the latter half of the century (Plate 46). Cornelis Dusart and Brakenburgh are representatives of the succeeding generation: in their works the peasant genre became overlaid with petit-bourgeois mannerism and pictorial style became a cultivated convention (Plates 47 and 48).

The pictures included in this volume represent three main periods.

At the centre of the first period is the Terbrugghen picture (Plate 1) dated 1623; included are earlier works, *A Merry Party* by Buytewech (Plates 4–5) and the painting by Dirck Hals (Plates 6–7); also later works, the panel by A. P. van de Venne (Plate 14), the picture by Andries Both (Plate 3) and *Peter's Denial of Christ* by Molenaer (Plates 9–10).

The second period begins with the picture attributed to Pieter de Molyn (Plates 17–18); more or less at the centre of this period comes Rembrandt's *Old Rabbi*, dated 1642 (Plate 27); also included are Benjamin Gerritsz. Cuyp's *Peasants in the Tavern* (Plate 20) and Adriaen van Ostade's *Interior with a Peasant Family* (Plate 23).

24

At the centre of the third period is Pieter de Hoogh's *Lady Reading a Letter* painted in 1664 (Plate 31) and, dating from the same year, the picture by Cornelis Bega (Plate 46); the paintings by Caspar Netscher (Plate 32), Gerbrand van den Eeckhout (Plate 30), Jan Steen (Plates 34–37) and Jacob Ochtervelt (Plate 38) are characteristic examples of the work of the third generation of genre painters.

# LITERATURE

For further reference concerning the paintings reproduced in this volume, see Pigler, Andor: *Országos Szépművészeti Múzeum. A régi Képtár katalógusa* (Museum of Fine Arts—Catalogue of the Old Picture Gallery), Vols. I and II, Budapest, 1954, where a complete bibliography of the paintings in the Museum of Fine Arts is to be found. For the Terbrugghen painting of the István Dobó Museum at Eger see Czobor, Ágnes: "Ein unbekanntes Bild des Hendrick Terbrugghen." *Oud Holland*, 1956, 229–232.

Additional standard works on the subject are:
Bode, W.: *Die Meister der holländischen und flämischen Malerschulen.* 8. Ausg. Neubearbeitet und ergänzt von E. Plietsch. Leipzig, 1956; Friedländer, J. M.: *Essays über die Landschaftsmalerei und andere Bildgattungen.* The Hague, 1947; Plietsch, E.: *Holländische und flämische Maler des XVII. Jahrhunderts*, Leipzig, 1960.

# LIST OF PLATES

PLATES

I

HENDRICK TERBRUGGHEN
Utrecht (1588–1629)

BOY LIGHTING A PIPE

István Dobó Museum, Eger, No. 55.236
Oil on canvas, 67.6 × 55 cm.
Signed right background: HTB 1623
From the Endre Pászthy Bequest

A pleasant-looking young soldier from the military barracks, sword on arm, is lighting his pipe from a candle which he has lifted out of the sconce in front of him. Two bright spheres of light are thrown over his face and shirt. The subject chosen by the artist is so simple, and at first sight so unambitious, that a contemporary viewer accustomed to formulas may well have sought for some abstruse meaning hidden beneath the apparent slightness of the theme. But the work demands no interpretation, only an appreciation of the episode depicted, and this simplicity is of pioneer significance in the development of genre painting. We learn from this picture that in Dutch genre it was not only everyday objects that came to be acceptable as subjects for paintings but also the unconscious and instinctive actions of men and women.

## 2

PIETER VAN LAER
(named Bamboccio in Rome), Haarlem (1592–1642)

## LANDSCAPE WITH MORRA-PLAYERS

Museum of Fine Arts, Budapest, No. 296
Oil on oak, 33.3 × 47 cm.
From the Esterházy Collection

Genre painters often represent some play or game. The simplest social game is the *morra* for which no objects are needed because the fingers of the hand suffice. This primitive entertainment has brought together this bunch of penniless, ragged tramps. Laer wilfully apprehended them and their environment in what they are common, trivial and humorous, too—unlike the other canvases of the painter. Aristocratic collectors liked such small-size genre pictures, for they considered them funny.

## 3

ANDRIES BOTH

Utrecht, later settled in Italy (1608–before 1649)

## Hunting by Candlelight

Museum of Fine Arts, Budapest, No. 382
Oil on canvas, 34.5 × 27 cm.
Signed to the left on the wall: ABoth 1630
From the Esterházy Collection

This is the earliest dated work of the artist, painted before he went to Italy. A ludicrous scene showing a peasant engrossed in the business of removing fleas from the body of a man kneeling half-clothed in front of him. A third peasant holds a candle to illuminate the operation while a fourth watches with close attention. This picture of peasant 'hunting' is just as successful as the artist's Romantic, Baroque scenes of the hunting parties of the aristocracy.

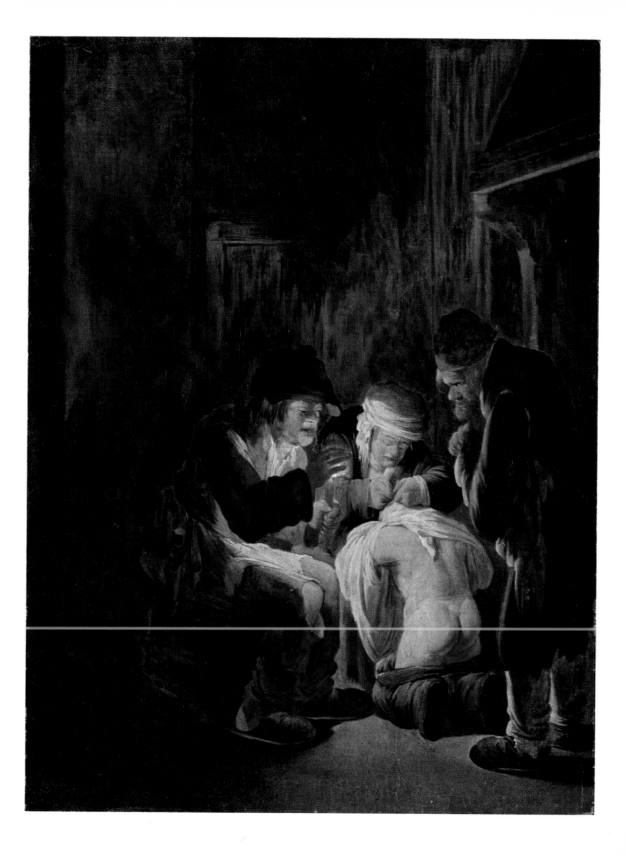

## 4

WILLEM PIETERSZ. BUYTEWECH
Rotterdam (1591/92–1624)

A MERRY PARTY

Museum of Fine Arts, Budapest, No. 3831
Canvas, 72.6×65.4 cm.
Purchased in 1908 from J. Goudstikker in Amsterdam. Painted around 1615

This is one of the earliest of the middle-class conversation pieces. It is typical of the early phase of Dutch genre painting, as can be seen from the limited amount of background, the figures made to turn so that they can be shown full face, the bright, emphatic and varied colours. A map and musical instruments hang on the wall behind the figures, on the floor are weapons, a metal jug and a goblet, while a tiny monkey balances on the chair. Together these objects create an atmosphere of physical and intellectual pleasure, and suggest the thrill of foreign travel and the conquest of distant lands.

WILLEM PIETERSZ. BUYTEWECH

A MERRY PARTY (detail)

DIRCK HALS
Haarlem (1591–1656)

## An Alfresco Party

Museum of Fine Arts, Budapest, No. 51.2878
Oil on oak, 34 × 61.3 cm.
Signed lower right on the chair: DHALS 1621
Acquired from the György Ráth Museum, Budapest, in 1949

Dirck Hals tried to emulate the fresh and casual style of his brother Frans, particularly in his spectacular way of painting, splendid clothes made of expensive fabrics. The colours are almost too vivid, like the early genre paintings. In this picture the festive party, seen against a background of columns and draperies on the left, seems to be momentarily frozen into a tableau in which the participants pose to welcome a new arrival—the spectator.

7

DIRCK HALS

An Alfresco Party (detail)

8

HARMEN HALS
Haarlem (1611–1669)

PEASANTS AT A WEDDING FEAST

Museum of Fine Arts, Budapest, No. 5166
Oil on oak, 58.6×91.5 cm.
Signed lower right on the barrel: HALS with interwoven letters
Presented by Hugo Kilényi in 1917

The drunken stupor of the figures in the foreground contrasts with the reeling movements of the figures still dancing in the background. The peasants are seen as ludicrous and insensitive creatures, capable only of the coarse amusements of the drunk.

9

JAN MIENSZ MOLENAER
Haarlem (*c.* 1610–1668)

PETER'S DENIAL OF CHRIST

Museum of Fine Arts, Budapest, No. 57.26
Oil on canvas, 99.5 × 135 cm.
Signed on the right side, on the back of the chair: M MOLENAER 1636
Purchased from Mrs. Richárd Tószeghy in 1957

This is a dramatic and colourful representation of a theme taken from the gospel. The detail is well observed. We are made to feel Peter's alarmed wish to escape and the scornful superiority of the servant-girl; we see the braggart, the sly informer and the soldiers, drunk and indifferent. It is as if the figures were characters in a biblical play produced to give the episode the tragi-comic casualness of everyday life. The style of the painting approaches so near to the developing tradition of contemporary genre that the religious theme is not immediately apparent. This picture exemplifies the moment in the development of the vigorous style of Dutch painting during the late sixteen-twenties and early sixteen-thirties when religious painting came closest to genre; from then onwards the two styles developed in ways that were mutually exclusive. Later, Rembrandt alone was to resolve the contradiction between the two styles, but his contemporaries, including Molenaer, all abandoned the attempt.

JAN MIENSZ MOLENAER

PETER'S DENIAL OF CHRIST (detail)

**I I**

JAN MIENSZ MOLENAER

## TAVERN OF THE CRESCENT MOON

Museum of Fine Arts, Budapest, No. 288
Oil on canvas, 87.8 × 102 cm.
Signed lower left on the fence: J Molenaer
From the Esterházy Collection

A family party sit in the open air round a table loaded with food and drink. A piper stands behind the table and plays for them. There is an atmosphere of enjoyment shared by everyone, the artisans and tradesmen, their wives, children and the old folk. The picture is carefully executed but there is a strange contrast between the painting of the figures, which are full of life, and the background of buildings and trees which has something of the unreality of a stage back-cloth. The artist shows more skill in his treatment of interiors.

JAN MIENSZ MOLENAER

## The Music-Makers

Museum of Fine Arts, Budapest, No. 53.495
Oil on canvas, 63 × 46 cm.
Signed to the right on the threshold: MOLENAER
From the collection of Count Jenő Zichy, acquired from the Budapest Municipal Gallery in 1953

In a plainly furnished room a young woman sits behind a table singing while the man sitting in the foreground plays a guitar. The colourful clothing of the music-makers, the still life composed by the objects on the table and the gently melancholic attitudes of the young people closeted together in this intimate corner of the room all contribute to the homely atmosphere of the picture.

13

JAN MIENSZ MOLENAER

PEASANTS IN THE TAVERN

Museum of Fine Arts, Budapest, No. 51.763
Oil on oak, 30.3 × 24.6 cm.
Signed below on the stone bench: J Molenaer
Acquired from the Ministry of Education in 1951

There is almost no detail depicted in the interior of the tavern where this group of peasants are shown drinking and enjoying themselves. The peasants are colourful, picturesque characters who with their coarse clothes have been grouped to make an effective composition.

## 14

ADRIAEN PIETERSZ. VAN DE VENNE
The Hague (1589–1662)

## "What Won't People Do for Money!"

Museum of Fine Arts, Budapest, No. 254
Oil on oak, 34.2 × 53 cm.
Signed lower left: Ad van de Venne f. 1625
Under the window runs the two-line legend: *Wat maeckmē al om gelt !*
Purchased from a private owner in 1882

The scene, which is no longer easy to define, ridicules greed for money, a favourite theme of this artist and one which he used in a number of paintings. The saying is simply portrayed, with no attempt to point the moral beyond what is implicit in the scene itself, which is depicted with all the jovial familiarity characteristic of the genre.

Wat maeckne
al ou gelt !

15

JACOB DUCK
Utrecht (*c.* 1600–after 1660)

## GUARDROOM WITH SOLDIERS PLAYING CARDS

Museum of Fine Arts, Budapest, No. 393
Oil on canvas, 42.5 × 36.3 cm.
From the Esterházy Collection

Although the soldiers are playing cards they are fully dressed, wearing hats and boots, their swords, breast-plates and banner in readiness beside them. The grey, undecorated walls of the guardroom suggest the discipline and boredom of their lives, the monotony of which can be relieved only by practice on the drum. The genre painters preferred not to show soldiers on guard—perhaps because they seemed ill at ease when performing this duty.

## 16

JAN OLIS
born at Gorinchem, active in Dordrecht (1610–1676)

## On Pleasure Bent

Museum of Fine Arts, Budapest, No. 51.785
Oil on oak, 49 × 63.5 cm.
Signed lower left, on the edge of the fireplace: JOlis fecit 1644
From the Ministry of Education in 1951

Seems to be a later and less significant variation of the Budapest picture by Buytewech (Plates 4–5), but here the party of men are seen in a much more humble and simply furnished place at amusement. Some of the men are smoking with evident enjoyment, but the party is not without an element of tediousness. The yellow, brownish-grey tones give a slightly metallic effect. The bright garments of the central figure, shown with his back to the onlooker, are in pronounced contrast to the plain dull colours worn by the other figures.

**17**

PIETER DE MOLYN (?)
Haarlem (1595–1661)

LANDSCAPE WITH PEASANTS CONVERSING

Museum of Fine Arts, Budapest, No. 1259
Oil on canvas, 90 × 98 cm.
Purchased from the Viennese art dealer Fr. Schwartz in 1896

Peasants returning from the fields have stopped for a moment by an old man sitting by the side of the road. The juxtaposition of young and old, which is a frequent motif in Dutch art, is in this case quite fortuitous. In fact the picture records a brief instant and is so generalized that it lacks all narrative quality. The painter expresses neither scorn, pity nor tenderness for his figures; his attitude is completely objective. Nevertheless the people portrayed are in one respect different from the tillers of the land usually seen in Dutch peasant genre: they are drawn on a larger scale. Here the landscape is less important than the figures and there is more attempt at characterization.

## 18

PIETER DE MOLYN (?)

LANDSCAPE WITH PEASANTS CONVERSING (detail)

19

JOOST CORNELISZ. DROOCHSLOOT
Utrecht (1586–1666)

VILLAGE STREET

Museum of Fine Arts, Budapest, No. 58.31
Oil on wood, 91.5 × 157 cm.
Signed lower left: J. Droochsloot 1654
Formerly in Count Jenő Zichy's Collection

An animated scene giving a general impression of the life of the village. The fact that everyone is out in the street seems to indicate that a holiday is in progress; the children are playing while the adults sit at the tables enjoying themselves. A crowd of beggars, cripples and others amuse themselves in the open space in front of the houses. The composition of the picture is rather loosely constructed indicating that the artist was attempting to capture the life of a village street in all its richness. No particular detail is allowed to hold the attention and there is no concentration of interest in any one aspect of the scene. The subject of the picture is the village itself and its inhabitants; it is a picture in which the crowd is more important than the individual.

## 20

BENJAMIN GERRITSZ. CUYP
Dordrecht (1612–1652)

## Peasants in the Tavern

Museum of Fine Arts, Budapest, No. 3825
Oil on oak, 53 × 76 cm.
Signed lower right on the wheel: Cvyp
Purchased from the Amsterdam art dealer J. Goudstikker in 1908

The tavern is ill-defined, though the rafters on both sides suggest a barn in which a group of men sit drinking and playing their instruments. The man sitting on the stool in the foreground, his long legs stretched in front of him, is playing the flute and the huge fat man facing him is playing the violin. The coarsely humorous faces are muddy-complexioned, as if to show that these men have some close affinity with their background of soil, straw and boards, all painted in similarly earthy colours.

## 21

ADRIAEN VAN OSTADE
Haarlem (1610–1684)

## The Quill-Sharpener

Museum of Fine Arts, Budapest, No. 286
Oil on oak, 33.2 × 26.7 cm.
The signature on the open book is no longer legible
From the Esterházy Collection

A man absorbed in the task of sharpening a quill is the subject of this excellent character study by Adriaen van Ostade, sometimes known as "the peasant Rembrandt." This is a genre picture in the same tradition as that by Terbrugghen showing a boy similarly engrossed in the task of lighting his pipe. This type of composition featuring only one figure, and usually only a part of that figure, is the simplest form of the genre: it would be impossible to depict a more limited aspect of the everyday movements of life.

## 22

ADRIAEN VAN OSTADE

FISHWIFE

Museum of Fine Arts, Budapest, No. 306
Oil on oak, 29 × 26.5 cm.
From the Esterházy Collection

The ugly face of this fat woman convinces one that she has spent all her life as a fishwife. She is framed by the outline of the market-stall with its board for a counter. Against this background of silver-scaled fish she herself looks like some frog-eyed creature, colourfully dressed for market. The picture is small but the artist has filled in a background depicting the teeming life of the market. Every detail, the display of fish, the figure behind the stall, the small building and the general view in the background together make up an animated scene which is captivating despite a complete absence of dramatic episodes, tension or humour.

## 23

ADRIAEN VAN OSTADE

## Interior with a Peasant Family

Museum of Fine Arts, Budapest, No. 4284
Oil on oak, 43.1 × 36.5 cm.
Signed lower right: A v Ostade 1647
Bequeathed by Count János Pálffy in 1912

The farmer stands by the table slicing bread, the little boy wearing a red cap is drinking soup, a second child is offering scraps to the dog, while the mother is busy with the baby of the family. The intimate family atmosphere is enriched by the subtle details of the setting which is splendidly painted in colours with transparent glazes. The peasants in this picture do not seem to be so poor and oppressed as those shown in other examples of the Dutch peasant genre; the home is comparatively well arranged and gives no suggestion of the hopelessness of a poverty-stricken life.

## 24

ISACK VAN OSTADE
Haarlem (1621–1649)

## The Slaughtered Pig

Museum of Fine Arts, Budapest, No. 55.373
Oil on oak, 41.5 × 30.7 cm
Originally in Count Jenő Zichy's collection, acquired from the Budapest Municipal Gallery

The children have retired to the corner of the peasant home to enjoy the minor pleasures of the pig-killing. On a frame propped against the flaking wall hangs the disembowelled carcass gleaming in the light, magnificently painted in yellowish-red flesh colours with transparent glazes. The bleeding flesh obtrudes like a banner against the picturesque, shabby interior. The picture reveals clearly the extent to which the artist was influenced by Rembrandt.

## 25

ISACK VAN OSTADE

## Pig-Killing

Museum of Fine Arts, Budapest, No. 282
Oil on oak, 39.8 × 53.8 cm.
Signed lower right: Isak van Ostade 1642
From the Esterházy Collection

The occupants of the one room which constitutes the peasant's home are busy as ants about the slaughtered pig. Their faces are scarcely discernible and the children can only be recognized by their smaller size and the fact that they are playing at blowing up the bladder. The adult figures are busy at the pump-well. All their world is within the confines of this one room which the artist has painted in a variety of browns and yellows, with which he has created a rather mysterious atmosphere.

## 26

ISACK VAN OSTADE

## Peasant Room

Museum of Fine Arts, Budapest, No. 292
Oil on oak, 44.6 × 39.5 cm.
Signed lower right: Isak van Ostade 1640
From the Esterházy Collection

This peasant room is warm and large like a barn and contains a collection of everything necessary for feeding men and animals. Basket, barrel, trough, broken jug, pail, ladder, tools and fodder have been hoarded by the farmer with all the collecting instinct of a hamster. He and his family are grouped round the fireplace trying to get warm, and the man's stance, though awkward, seems to indicate that he is master of his rather poor house. The colours are all different shades of brown and yellow.

## 27

REMBRANDT HARMENSZ. VAN RYN
Leiden and later Amsterdam (1606–1669)

OLD RABBI

Museum of Fine Arts, Budapest, No. 235
Oil on oak, 70.5 × 53.5 cm.
Signed on lower left: Rembrandt f. 1642
From the Esterházy Collection

The seated figure of a wise old man is outlined against an obscure background, his face and hands brightly illuminated by the light from a candle. It is a pose frequently seen in seventeenth-century portraits and one frequently used by Rembrandt himself. Although this is a portrait from life, the treatment of the subject evokes a biblical atmosphere. The picture is almost allegorical: the old man's attitude of meditation symbolizes the ephemeral nature of man's intellect. The light shining on his face is echoed in the glow from the back and the copper candlestick, familiar objects that give a feeling of warm intimacy. The picture was painted in the same year as the famous *Night Watch*.

## 28

GERRIT DOU
Leiden (1613–1675)

## An Officer of the Leiden Civic Guard

Museum of Fine Arts, Budapest, No. 62.10
Oil on oak, 66 × 51 cm.
Purchased from Dr. Zsigmond Jakabházy in 1962

The cavernous background gives an immediate impression of a ship's hold but there is all the detail of a still life in the carefully painted armour, drum, saddle and guns seen in what must be an arsenal. It is only the figure of the officer with his plumed headband which makes this a genre painting. Like most of Dou's works this picture is quite lacking in incident. The man is no more than a carefully painted object included in the picture along with the rest of the contents of the store-room.

## 29

JAN VICTORS
Amsterdam (about 1620–1676 or later)

MARKET SCENE WITH A QUACK AT HIS STALL

Museum of Fine Arts, Budapest, No. 1331
Oil on canvas, 79 × 99 cm.
Signed lower right on the foot-stool: iohanes Victors
Purchased from the London art dealer P. D. Colnaghi in 1894

The market-place is in fact limited to the quack's table with an awning over it, and the group of simple people crowding round the stall. The church and houses round the market-square are outlined behind the group of onlookers and the village street with figures can be seen in the distance. The peasant sitting barefooted, one of his shoes discarded beside him, the charlatan in his finery, and the colourful company of villagers around them are characters in an anecdotical story which is indeed worthy of the painter's brush. Victors was a pupil of Rembrandt, and his figures are clearly derivative but they are smooth and superficial compared with the character studies of the great master.

## 30

GERBRAND VAN DEN EECKHOUT
Amsterdam (1621–1674)

## SCHOLAR WITH HIS BOOKS

Museum of Fine Arts, Budapest, No. 5985
Oil on oak, 64.5 × 49 cm.
Signed lower right: G. V. Eeckhout 1671
Bequeathed by Count Miklós Széchenyi in 1924

Eeckhout's *Scholar with his Books* gives us no impression of the wisdom evoked in Rembrandt's portrait of the *Old Rabbi*. Here we see an industrious pedant whose learning is indicated only by external objects—the books and the globe. The learned men portrayed by Vermeer and Rembrandt are men of exceptional qualities but their portraits cannot be called genre paintings. This picture by Eeckhout is certainly a genre painting, the sitter, however, is not shown to be a sage but a burgher. The warm brownish-red and yellowish colours and the manner of painting are reminiscent of Rembrandt's later style.

## 31

PIETER DE HOOGH
Delft and The Hague (1629–1683)

## LADY READING A LETTER

Museum of Fine Arts, Budapest, No. 5933
Oil on canvas, 55 × 55 cm
Signed lower right: P. de Hoogh 1664
Purchased from a private owner in Budapest in 1923

The sunlight streaming through the window suggests early afternoon. Reflected light and soft shadows are intermingled on the oriental rug spread over the table, the leather-backed chairs, the curtain and the lead-framed window-panes. It seems as if the quiet would be hardly broken by any sounds from far or near. The act of reading by the young woman sitting in a corner of the room is just as objectively portrayed, and there is no more suggestion of a unique experience than there was in *Boy Lighting a Pipe*, *The Quill-Sharpener* or some of the other genre paintings in this volume. The atmosphere of intimacy is absolute, emanating alike from the lady and the objects included in the composition.

## 32

CASPAR NETSCHER
The Hague (1639–1684)

PRESENTATION OF THE MEDALLION

Museum of Fine Arts, Budapest, No. 250
Oil on canvas, 62 × 67.5 cm.
Signed on the right, on the cupboard: C. Netscher 16...
From the Esterházy Collection

A young officer kneels to present a medallion to a young woman sitting by a table. She receives his attentions with no show of emotion, unlike the woman behind her and the young man beside her who are preparing to drink a toast. A feature of this work is the splendid painting of the elaborate costumes worn by the protagonists. It is not possible, nor is it important, to decide whether the officer is making a declaration of love or merely handing over the medallion on behalf of some absent friend.

## 33

CORNELIS DE MAN
Delft (1621–1706)

## The Chess Players

Museum of Fine Arts, Budapest, No. 320
Oil on canvas, 97.5 × 85 cm.
Signed lower right: CDMan
From the Esterházy Collection

A homely room in which a well-groomed gentleman and an elegantly gowned lady are playing chess. The cat, logs and bellows near the hearth all contribute to the atmosphere of pleasant domesticity which is somewhat marred by the man's affected gestures and the woman's backward glance at the onlooker. The placing of the hands and figures is rather artificial in its ingenuity but the painting of the curtains and the other fabrics is superbly realistic.

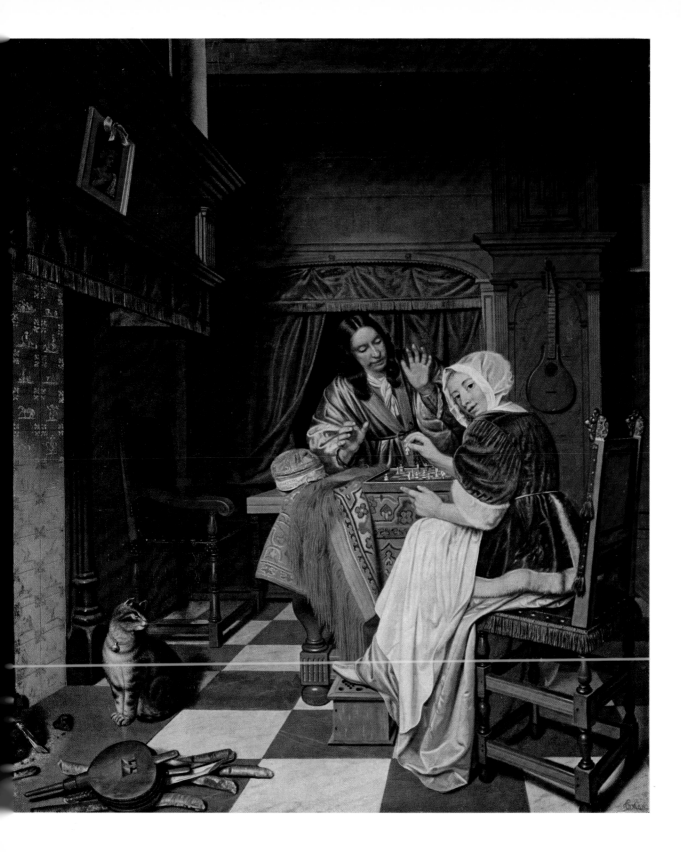

JAN STEEN
Leiden (1626–1679)

## THE CAT FAMILY

Museum of Fine Arts, Budapest, No. 337
Oil on canvas, 150 × 148 cm.
Signed lower left: J. Steen
From the Esterházy Collection

This picture splendidly summarizes the art of Steen—and Dutch genre as a whole. The centre of the family circle is the cat family in the basket on the table. Everybody is happy, gay and completely relaxed. The artist indicates our senses as the main source of pleasure: hearing makes us enjoy music; the sense of touch enables us to enjoy stroking the cats; the sense of taste and smell are satisfied by drinking; and our sight conveys the delight of reading an amusing story. The latter joy is represented by the figure of the artist himself, for the reader is a self-portrait. The pleasing figure of a woman seen with her back to the onlooker could be the pleasure-giving muse of genre painting—if genre painting ever had such a muse. And if there were no such muse, then she must be considered to be Steen's most captivating figure of a woman, whose face, however, was apparently not worthy of the painter's brush.

35     JAN STEEN

THE CAT FAMILY (detail)

JAN STEEN

THE CAT FAMILY (detail)

JAN STEEN

## A Welcome for the Visitor

Museum of Fine Arts, Budapest, No. 4300
Oil on oak, 61.6 × 46 cm.
Signed on the right, above the door: IAN. STEEN
Bequeathed by Count János Pálffy in 1912

The voluptuous lady leaning back with one elbow resting on a cushion, wineglass in hand, expects payment from her visitor: the young man at the door is giving money to the old woman leaning on her stick. There is a discreetly curtained bed in the corner of the room and on the wall a picture in which one figure is seen driving a second from an open doorway. The details have been carefully observed and the whole scene depicted with irony. The picture is a splendid example of Steen's later period.

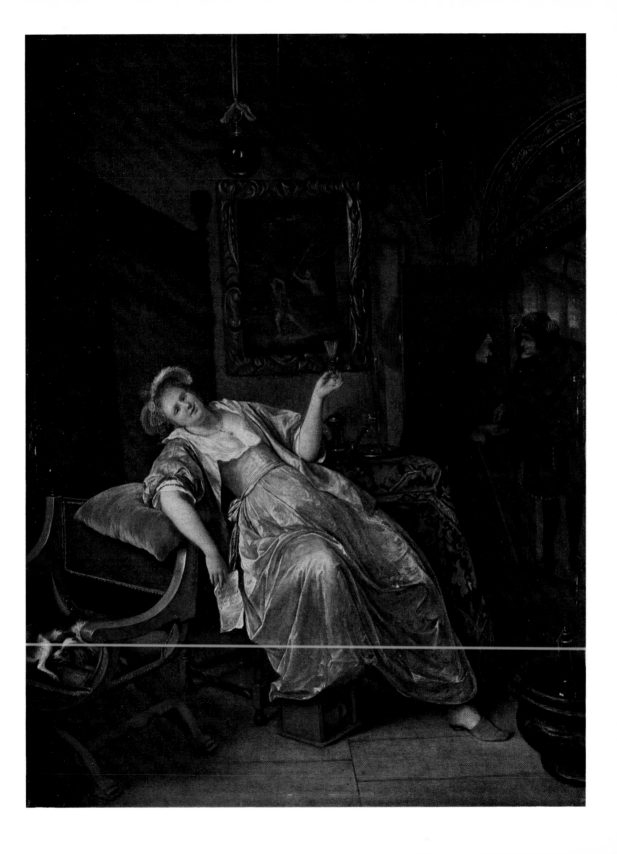

## 38

JACOB OCHTERVELT
Rotterdam and later Amsterdam (1634/35–1708/10)

## A Family Group

Museum of Fine Arts, Budapest, No. 4286
Oil on canvas, 96.5 × 91 cm.
Signed above the door to the left: Jac.° Ochtervelt. f. A.° 1670.
Bequeathed by Count János Pálffy in 1912

A middle-class family is shown stiffly posed for a group portrait in a rather bare but impressive hall. The glossy white and yellow satin frocks of the two girls and the combination of brown, grey and black herald the colour fashions which later dominated the *Feinmalerei* period of genre. The forms are clean-cut and as smooth and polished as if they had been turned on a lathe.

## 39

PHILIPS WOUWERMAN
Haarlem (1619–1668)

## The Manège

Museum of Fine Arts, Budapest, No. 304
Oil on canvas, 68 × 83 cm.
Initials on the back of the horse to the right: PHSW
From the Esterházy Collection

A company of horse trainers are seen in a woodland glade in the mountains breaking in horses. In this composition the figures of the riders, grooms and children, all clothed in bright colour, are no more important than the horses. The trees, billowing cumulus clouds and rather misty landscape suggest a more southerly setting than the place where this picture was in fact painted. The prancing movements of the saddled horses make this an exceptionally animated composition.

## 40

DIRK MAAS
Haarlem (1659–1717)

## ITALIAN MARKET-PLACE

Museum of Fine Arts, Budapest, No. 275
Oil on canvas, 68 × 81 cm.
Signed lower right: D. maas
From the Esterházy Collec.ion

A fair is being held in the market-place of an Italian city. The scene provides a medley of colours from the elaborate clothes of the salesmen and customers and all the horses of different breeds. Above the crowds and tents a globe can be seen on top of a high column, and riding the globe sits Mercury, the god of commerce. A counterpart of this picture, representing a horse fair, is also in the Museum of Fine Arts in Budapest.

**41**

DOMINICUS VAN WYNEN (ASCANIUS)
Amsterdam (1661–1690)

## Don Quixote at the Inn (Cervantes, *D. Qu.*, I, Chapter 45)

Museum of Fine Arts, Budapest, No. 221
Oil on canvas, 73 × 93.5 cm.
Signed lower left: DW. ASCANIUS
Presented by Dr. Károly Pulszky

This picture exemplifies a happy union between the chivalry, romance and humour of the romantic school and the everyday reality of the genre. Such unions are rare and it is interesting and instructive to note that it is in a Dutch painting that we find the clearest expression of the humour of the Spanish literary masterpiece. The picture illustrates the whirlwind of comedy arising from the discovery that Don Quixote's copper 'helmet' is really a barber's copping bowl and the plotters' attempt to make out that the donkey's saddle is the knight's mount.

DOMINICUS VAN WYNEN (ASCANIUS)

DON QUIXOTE AT THE INN (detail)

43 DOMINICUS VAN WYNEN (ASCANIUS)

Don Quixote at the Inn (detail)

## 44

THOMAS WYCK
Haarlem (*c.* 1616–1647)

## Italian Port

Museum of Fine Arts, Budapest, No. 64.5
Oil on canvas, 81 × 100 cm.
Initials on the central box: T. W.
Purchased from Vilmos Feldmetter in 1964

There is something unmistakably Dutch in the portrayal of the figures and the painting of the scene on the wharf although the fortress walls and the view beyond give the impression of Italian landscape, which the painter must in fact have seen. Though the style of the scene on the wharf may be essentially Dutch yet the very fact of representing it reflects Italian influence, for Dutch painters rarely painted harbour scenes or any kind of commercial activity at home, whereas during their sojourns in Italy they learned to appreciate the attraction of market-places and lost some of their interest in interiors. This picture is one of the artist's most significant works.

THOMAS WYCK

ITALIAN PORT (detail)

CORNELIS BEGA
Haarlem (1620–1664)

## TAVERN SCENE

Museum of Fine Arts, Budapest, No. 4299
Oil on canvas, 48.6 × 41.5 cm.
Signed on lower right: C Bega 1664
Bequeathed by Count János Pálffy in 1912

Cornelis Bega painted this picture twenty years before the death of his master Adriaen van Ostade. His peasants are shown with more detail than those in the work of the van Ostade brothers; in this picture, for instance, they are shown stupid with liquor, bragging and flirting with the barmaid. They are painted with graphic skill but the style of painting is rather monotonous. Bega was merely a popular practitioner while the van Ostade brothers were classic interpreters of Dutch peasant genre.

47 CORNELIS DUSART
Haarlem (1660–1704)

TAVERN SCENE

Museum of Fine Arts, Budapest, No. 283
Oil on canvas, 68.3 × 57 cm.
Signed lower left: Dusart fec.
From the Esterházy Collection

Compared with the destitute-looking peasant interiors seen in earlier works, this tavern is bright and well-arranged. The peasants are seen eating, drinking and enjoying themselves and they are more carefully dressed than the figures in earlier peasant scenes. Even the gestures of these peasants have been made to look distinguished, but the result is to make them more ordinary and less interesting than the figures in van Ostade's paintings.

RICHARD BRAKENBURGH
Haarlem (1650–1702)

MERRYMAKERS

Museum of Fine Arts, Budapest, No. 259
Oil on canvas, 76×91 cm.
Signed lower left: R. Brackenbourgh. f.
From the Esterházy Collection

The light is beginning to fade in a room where a number of men of the lower middle classes
have been dallying with doll-faced ladies of easy virtue. The merrymaking has probably reached
its climax, as shown by the various objects scattered over the foreground, yet the lecherous
old men and the young men too, seem to be still dull. Like most of the examples of later
genre, the composition, colouring and light effects are by no means satisfactory: in this work
we can sense that the great period of Dutch genre is beginning to decline.